COPYWRITING SECRETS

Crafting Compelling Content for Impactful
Results

Written By: Asif Mehmood

Table of Contents

1. Introduction to Copywriting 1-3

2. Understanding Your Audience 3-5

3. Crafting Captivating Headlines 6-8

4. The Power of Persuasion in Copy............................8-10

5. Structuring Engaging Copy: From
    AIDA to Storytelling...10-13

6. Copywriting for Different Platforms (Web,
    Social Media, Print)... 13-16

7. SEO and Copywriting: Writing for Visibility 16-19

8. Testing and Refining Your Copy........................... 19-22

9. Conclusion 22-23

Introduction

Welcome to "Copywriting Secrets: The Art and Science of Compelling Content." In this comprehensive guide, we'll delve deep into the world of copywriting, exploring its nuances, strategies, and techniques that transform ordinary content into persuasive, engaging, and impactful copy. Good copywriting isn't merely about words; it's about understanding human psychology, consumer behavior, and the art of communication. This book is designed to equip you with the knowledge and skills necessary to become a proficient copywriter, capable of capturing attention, stirring emotions, and driving desired actions through your words.

Throughout these chapters, you'll journey from the fundamentals of copywriting to advanced strategies, learning how to tailor your message to different audiences, leverage psychological triggers, optimize for search engines, and continuously refine your approach to achieve optimal results.

Whether you're a seasoned marketer looking to refine your skills or a newcomer eager to explore the world of persuasive writing, this book aims to be your comprehensive guide, offering practical insights, real-world examples, and actionable steps to elevate your copywriting prowess.

Chapter 1:

Introduction to Copywriting Secrets, the art of crafting compelling and persuasive content, stands as the cornerstone of effective communication in the realm of marketing and advertising. It serves as the bridge between brands and their audiences, wielding the power to captivate, persuade, and ultimately drive actions.

Defining Copywriting:

At its essence, copywriting revolves around the strategic use of words to evoke emotions, convey messages, and prompt specific responses from the intended audience. It goes beyond the mere arrangement of sentences; it's the strategic orchestration of language to achieve predefined objectives, whether it's to sell a product, inspire engagement, or inform and educate.

Significance in Marketing:

In the vast landscape of marketing, copywriting emerges as a linchpin. It forms the soul of advertisements, website content, social media posts, email campaigns, and every medium that demands communication. A well-crafted copy has the potential to transform a business's presence, cultivating brand loyalty, and sparking conversions.

Influence on Consumer Behavior:

Understanding consumer psychology lies at the heart of effective copywriting. By comprehending the desires, pain points, motivations, and aspirations of the target audience, copywriters tailor messages that resonate deeply. This understanding enables them to create content that not only attracts attention but also compels action.

Evolution of Copywriting:

The evolution of copywriting mirrors the evolution of human communication itself. From the days of print ads and billboards to the digital age dominated by websites, social media, and video content, copywriting techniques have adapted and expanded. However, certain foundational principles remain timeless—connecting emotionally, offering solutions, and being persuasive.

Distinction Between Copy and Content:

While often used interchangeably, copy and content serve distinct purposes. Content is informative, entertaining, or educational material aimed at engaging an audience, whereas copy is specifically designed to prompt action. Whether it's making a purchase, signing up for a newsletter, or clicking a link, copy is crafted with a clear call-to-action in mind.

Primary Goals of Copywriting:

The primary goals of copywriting revolve around grabbing attention, generating interest, creating desire, and compelling action—the AIDA model (Attention, Interest, Desire, Action). Every piece of copy aims to guide the reader through these stages, nudging them towards a specific outcome.

Chapter 2:

Understanding Your Audience In the world of copywriting, success hinges upon a deep understanding of the audience you're communicating with. Every word, phrase, and narrative crafted in copy should resonate with the intended audience to evoke the desired response. Understanding your audience isn't just about demographics; it's about comprehending their desires, fears, aspirations, and behavioral patterns.

Defining Your Target Audience:

Identifying your target audience involves more than categorizing them by age, gender, location, or income. It's about creating detailed personas that encapsulate the psychographics, interests, values, and pain points of your ideal customers. This goes beyond superficial traits and delves into their motivations, preferences, and decision-making processes.

Conducting Research:

Thorough research is the bedrock of audience understanding. Utilize surveys, interviews, social media analytics, and market research to gather insights. Dive into online forums, social media groups, and discussions relevant to your niche to understand the language, concerns, and sentiments of your audience firsthand.

Creating Empathy Maps:

Empathy maps are invaluable tools in deciphering audience behavior. They visually represent the thoughts, feelings, actions, and pain points of your audience segments. By mapping out what your audience hears, sees, thinks, and feels, you gain a holistic view that guides your copywriting strategy.

Tailoring Messages to Resonate:

Once armed with comprehensive audience insights, tailor your messages to resonate deeply. Speak their language, address their concerns, and align your brand's values with theirs. The goal is to create a connection that goes beyond surface-level engagement, fostering a sense of understanding and trust.

Utilizing Psychographic Segmentation:

Beyond demographics, psychographic segmentation divides audiences based on attitudes, beliefs, and lifestyle choices. Understanding the psychographics helps in crafting copy that speaks directly to the values and aspirations of specific segments, enhancing the relevance and impact of your message.

Feedback and Adaptation:

Effective understanding of your audience is an ongoing process. Collect feedback, analyze the performance of your copy, and adapt your approach accordingly. Embrace a dynamic strategy that evolves alongside your audience's changing preferences and behaviors.

Chapter 3: Crafting Captivating Headlines

The Art of Headline Creation:

Headlines serve as the gateway to your content, wielding immense power to entice readers to delve deeper. Crafting headlines that stand out amidst the digital noise requires a delicate blend of art and science. This chapter navigates through the strategies and techniques essential for creating headlines that not only grab attention but also resonate with your audience.

Understanding the Audience's Needs and Desires:

Effective headlines address the audience's pain points, desires, and curiosities. They promise solutions, insights, or entertainment, aligning with what the audience seeks. Analyzing audience personas and conducting thorough research helps tailor headlines that directly appeal to their motivations.

Embracing Emotional Triggers:

Emotions play a pivotal role in compelling readers to engage. Headlines infused with emotion—whether it's humor, curiosity, fear, or excitement—tug at the reader's heartstrings, drawing them into the content. This chapter dissects how different emotional triggers can be strategically utilized to craft powerful headlines.

Leveraging the Power of Numbers and Statistics:

Numerical figures have a magnetic pull in headlines. They promise concrete and specific information, making the content appear structured and valuable. Learning how to incorporate numbers effectively—be it in lists, statistics, or percentages—can significantly enhance the headline's appeal.

Employing Persuasive Language and Triggers:

The choice of words in a headline can make a substantial difference. This chapter explores the use of persuasive language, including power words, calls-to-action, and trigger words, to create urgency and compel readers to take action.

Crafting Variations and Testing:

Crafting multiple headline variations and conducting A/B testing is a fundamental practice. Analyzing which headlines perform best in terms of engagement, click-through rates, and conversions helps refine your headline-writing skills and understand your audience's preferences better.

The Role of Headlines Across Platforms:

Headlines differ in their effectiveness based on the platform they're presented on. Understanding the nuances of crafting headlines for social media, blog posts, email subjects, and more is crucial for maximizing engagement on each platform.

Chapter 4: The Power of Persuasion in Copy

Understanding Psychological Triggers:

Persuasion isn't merely convincing; it's about understanding human behavior and leveraging psychological triggers to influence actions. This chapter delves into the fundamental principles that underpin persuasive copywriting.

Social Proof and Authority:

Harnessing social proof—showcasing endorsements, testimonials, or social validation—builds trust and credibility. Additionally, establishing authority through expertise, credentials, or endorsements from reputable sources lends weight to your copy, nudging readers towards action.

Scarcity and Urgency:

Creating a sense of scarcity or urgency prompts immediate action. Limited-time offers, exclusive deals, or limited stock notices activate the fear of missing out (FOMO) in readers, compelling them to act swiftly to avoid losing the opportunity.

The Art of Storytelling:

Storytelling weaves an emotional connection between the audience and the message. Through narratives that resonate with the audience's experiences, aspirations, or challenges, copywriters can evoke empathy and inspire action. Stories have the power to captivate, engage, and persuade like no other technique.

Consistency and Commitment:

Encouraging small commitments or actions creates a path towards larger commitments. By employing techniques that lead readers to agree or commit to smaller actions, such as signing up for a newsletter or a free trial, copywriters can pave the way for more substantial conversions.

Reciprocity and Value Exchange:

Offering value before expecting anything in return fosters reciprocity. Providing useful content, free resources, or valuable insights establishes a sense of indebtedness in the audience, increasing the likelihood of them reciprocating by engaging or making a purchase.

Ethical Application of Persuasive Techniques:

While persuasive techniques are powerful, ethical considerations are paramount. This chapter emphasizes the responsible use of these tools to genuinely benefit the audience. Building trust and long-term relationships with the audience should always remain the primary focus.

Chapter 5: Structuring Engaging Copy: From AIDA to Storytelling

Crafting a Journey through Copy:

Effective copywriting isn't just about words; it's about guiding the audience through a journey that captivates their attention, stirs their interest, evokes desire, and ultimately prompts action. This chapter dissects the AIDA model and the impactful role of storytelling in achieving these objectives.

AIDA Model: Attention, Interest, Desire, Action:

The AIDA model serves as a blueprint for structuring copy that guides readers seamlessly through stages. Attention involves captivating the audience from the outset. Interest sustains engagement by piquing curiosity and providing valuable information. Desire cultivates emotional connections, making readers yearn for the benefits offered. Finally, a clear Call-to-Action prompts the desired response.

Attention-Grabbing Headlines and Openings:

To initiate the AIDA cycle, attention-grabbing headlines and compelling openings are paramount. Techniques like posing questions, utilizing shocking statistics, or offering intriguing statements serve to hook the audience, urging them to delve deeper into the content.

Sustaining Interest with Engaging Content:

Maintaining interest requires delivering content that aligns with audience needs and preferences. Providing valuable information, addressing pain points, and presenting solutions sustains engagement, keeping readers invested in the narrative.

Evoking Desire through Emotional Connection:

Creating desire involves connecting emotionally with the audience. Storytelling emerges as a powerful tool here, enabling copywriters to craft narratives that resonate deeply. By highlighting benefits, painting vivid scenarios, or showcasing success stories, the copy stirs emotions and fosters desire for the offered solution or product.

Compelling Calls-to-Action for Actionable Results:

The culmination of the AIDA cycle, the Call-to-Action, must be clear, persuasive, and action-oriented. Whether it's making a purchase, subscribing, or engaging further, a compelling CTA prompts readers to take the desired action.

The Art of Storytelling:

Storytelling transcends the AIDA model, enriching copy by creating emotional connections. Through narratives that resonate with human experiences, aspirations, or challenges, copywriters can captivate audiences, fostering deeper engagement and alignment with the message.

Seamlessly Integrating AIDA and Storytelling:

The marriage of the AIDA model and storytelling techniques results in powerful, engaging copy. By strategically structuring content to progress through AIDA stages while incorporating storytelling elements, copywriters can create compelling narratives that resonate emotionally and guide readers organically towards action.

Chapter 6: Copywriting for Different Platforms (Web, Social Media, Print)

Adapting Copy to Diverse Platforms:

Copywriting isn't one-size-fits-all; it requires adaptation to suit the distinct demands of various mediums. This chapter delves into the nuances of crafting effective copy for different platforms, acknowledging the unique characteristics and expectations of each.

Social Media: Concise and Impactful Messaging:

Social media demands brevity and impact. Crafting copy for platforms like Twitter, Instagram, or TikTok requires condensing messages while maintaining attention-grabbing content. Embracing hashtags, visuals, and concise yet compelling copy is vital to captivate scrolling audiences.

Web Content: SEO-Driven and Informative:

Writing for the web involves catering to both human readers and search engines. SEO techniques — incorporating keywords naturally, optimizing meta descriptions, and ensuring readability—are essential. Informative, engaging content that provides value while adhering to SEO guidelines is key for web copywriting.

Print: Descriptive and Visually Evocative:

Print mediums allow for more descriptive and visually evocative content. Brochures, magazines, or flyers provide space for detailed descriptions and captivating visuals. Copywriters leverage storytelling, vivid language, and compelling imagery to engage readers in print formats.

Email Marketing: Personalized and Action-Oriented:

Email copywriting involves personalized messages tailored to specific audiences. Crafting subject lines that entice opens and content that prompts action—whether it's making a purchase, signing up, or engaging further—is crucial. Building trust and offering value are central to successful email copy.

Video and Audio Scripts: Conversational and Engaging:

Copywriting for video or audio scripts requires a conversational tone that engages audiences. Whether for YouTube, podcasts, or commercials, the script's flow, language, and narrative drive engagement and maintain interest throughout the audio-visual experience.

Adaptation and Consistency Across Platforms:

Maintaining brand voice and consistency across platforms is essential. While adapting to the unique demands of each platform, ensuring a coherent brand identity fosters familiarity and trust among audiences encountering the brand in diverse contexts.

Understanding Platform - Specific Expectations:

Each platform has its own etiquette, character limits, visual requirements, and audience behaviors. Understanding these platform-specific nuances empowers copywriters to tailor content that resonates effectively and maximizes engagement.

Chapter 7: SEO and Copywriting: Writing for Visibility

The Crucial Bond between SEO and Copy:

Search Engine Optimization (SEO) and copywriting go hand in hand to ensure content visibility and reach. This chapter emphasizes the integration of SEO strategies into copywriting, harmonizing the needs of both readers and search engines.

Keyword Integration: Balancing Relevance and Natural Flow:

Incorporating keywords seamlessly into copy is essential. Striking a balance between keyword relevance and the natural flow of content ensures readability while signaling to search engines the topical relevance of the content.

Optimizing Meta Descriptions and Title Tags:

Crafting compelling meta descriptions and title tags is an art. These snippets serve as a preview of content in search engine results. Optimizing them with relevant keywords and enticing language increases click-through rates while providing concise summaries of the content.

Creating High-Quality, Valuable Content:

Quality content reigns supreme in SEO. Copywriters must focus on providing value to readers through informative, engaging, and well-researched content. Understanding user intent and addressing their queries comprehensively elevates content quality, improving its ranking potential.

User Experience and Readability:

SEO isn't just about keywords; it's also about user experience. Copywriters should prioritize readability, using headings, bullet points, and clear structures to enhance content accessibility. Ensuring mobile responsiveness and fast-loading pages further contributes to a positive user experience.

Link Building and Authority:

Earning quality backlinks from reputable sources strengthens a website's authority and credibility. Creating valuable content that naturally attracts links is pivotal. Additionally, internal linking within content aids in navigation and strengthens the site's structure.

Analytics and Continuous Improvement:

Utilizing analytics tools to track performance metrics is crucial. Monitoring rankings, click-through rates, bounce rates, and engagement metrics helps in understanding content performance. This data-driven approach enables continuous refinement and optimization of copywriting strategies.

Ethical SEO Practices:

Adhering to ethical SEO practices is paramount. Avoiding keyword stuffing, cloaking, or other black hat techniques preserves credibility and sustains long-term success in search engine rankings.

Chapter 8: Testing and Refining Your Copy

The Iterative Nature of Compelling Copy:

Crafting compelling copy isn't a one-time task; it's an ongoing process of refinement and improvement. This chapter underscores the significance of testing various methodologies and leveraging feedback to continuously enhance the impact and relevance of your content.

A/B Testing for Comparative Analysis:

A/B testing involves presenting variations of content to different audiences to determine which performs better. Comparing different headlines, calls-to-action, or content structures helps identify elements that resonate most effectively with the audience, optimizing for engagement and conversions.

User Feedback and Surveys:

Direct feedback from users provides invaluable insights. Surveys, feedback forms, or user testing sessions offer qualitative data about audience preferences, pain points, and opinions. Understanding audience perspectives helps tailor content to meet their needs more effectively.

Analyzing Performance Metrics:

Metrics such as click-through rates, conversion rates, time on page, or bounce rates offer quantitative data on content performance. Analyzing these metrics provides a clear understanding of how audiences interact with the content, guiding adjustments to improve its effectiveness.

Continuous Adaptation and Improvement:

The key to success lies in continual adaptation. Implementing changes based on testing outcomes and feedback ensures that content remains relevant and impactful in the ever-evolving landscape. Iterative improvements maintain audience engagement and drive desired actions.

Multivariate Testing for Deeper Insights:

Beyond A/B testing, multivariate testing assesses multiple variables simultaneously. This method enables a more comprehensive understanding of how different combinations of elements impact audience behavior, providing deeper insights for refinement.

Incorporating Data-Driven Decisions:

Data-driven decisions steer content refinement. By amalgamating qualitative and quantitative data, copywriters can make informed decisions to tweak elements, refine messaging, or adjust strategies to optimize content performance.

Embracing Flexibility and Adaptability:

Embracing flexibility allows for swift adaptation to changing audience preferences or market trends. This agility enables copywriters to stay ahead by swiftly adjusting content strategies based on emerging data and evolving audience behavior.

The Continuous Cycle of Improvement:

The refinement of copywriting is an unending cycle. Embracing testing, feedback, and data-driven iterations leads to perpetual enhancements, ensuring that content remains relevant, engaging, and aligned with audience expectations.

Conclusion:

In the journey through the pages of "Copywriting Secrets," we've delved deep into the intricate world of crafting compelling content. From understanding the nuances of audience psychology to mastering the art of persuasive language, this book has served as a guide illuminating the pathways to impactful copywriting.

Throughout these chapters, we've uncovered the significance of attention-grabbing headlines that captivate, narratives that resonate emotionally, and calls-to-action that prompt desired responses. We've navigated the terrain of SEO optimization, adapting to diverse platforms, and harnessing the psychology behind persuasive techniques. But beyond the strategies and techniques lies a fundamental truth: the power of words to influence, connect, and inspire action. Copywriting isn't merely about arranging sentences; it's about weaving stories that evoke emotions, providing solutions that resonate, and establishing connections that endure. As we conclude this journey, armed with insights, tools, and strategies, remember that the magic of copywriting lies in its ability to bridge the gap between brands and their audiences. It's about forging relationships, sparking conversations, and driving meaningful engagement.

Whether you're a seasoned marketer seeking to refine your skills or a novice eager to unlock the secrets of persuasive writing, may the knowledge gained from "Copywriting Secrets" empower you to craft content that not only informs but compels, not only communicates but resonates, and ultimately, drives the results you seek.